THE HOME FRONT
OF THE REVOLUTIONARY WAR

PATRICK CATEL

Heinemann Library
Chicago, Illinois

www.heinemannraintree.com
Visit our website to find out
more information about
Heinemann-Raintree books.

To order:

☎ Phone 888-454-2279
💻 Visit www.heinemannraintree.com
to browse our catalog and order online.

Edited by Megan Cotugno
Designed by Ryan Frieson
Picture research by Tracy Cummins
Originated by Capstone Global Library
Printed in the USA by Lake Book Manufacturing Inc.

14 13 12 11 10
10 9 8 7 6 5 4 3 2 1

Library of Congress Cataloging-in-Publication Data

Catel, Patrick.
  The home front of the Revolutionary War / Patrick Catel.
    p. cm. — (Why we fought : the Revolutionary War)
  Includes bibliographical references and index.
  ISBN 978-1-4329-3895-6 (hardcover)
  1. United States—History—Revolution, 1775-1783—Social
aspects--Juvenile literature. 2. United States—Social life and
customs--1775-1783—Juvenile literature. 3. United States—
Social conditions—To 1865--Juvenile literature. I. Title.
  E209.C365 2011
  973.3'1—dc22
                        2009051089

Acknowledgments

The author and publishers are grateful to the following for
permission to reproduce copyright material:

Corbis pp. 13 (© Hulton-Deutsch Collection), 32 (©
Bettmann), 37 (© Corbis), 40 (© Bettmann); Getty Images
p. 39 (National Geographic); Library of Congress Prints and
Photographs Division pp. 4, 11, 14, 20, 25, 27, 29, 33, 34,
36, 41; NARA p. 24 (War and Conflict CD); National Park
Service p. 12 (Colonial National Historical Park); North
Wind Picture Archives pp. 19, 23 (© North Wind); The Art
Archive pp. 10, 18, 43 (Culver Pictures); The Bridgeman Art
Library International p. 16 (© Christie's Images); The Granger
Collection, New York pp. 7, 8, 9, 15, 17, 30, 35, 38, 42.

Cover photo of Bostonians on their housetops watching
the Battle of Bunker's Hill at Charlestown on June 17, 1775.
Illustration, 1901, by Howard Pyle reproduced with permission
from The Granger Collection, New York.

We would like to thank Dr. Edward Cook for his invaluable
help in the preparation of this book.

Every effort has been made to contact copyright holders of
any material reproduced in this book. Any omissions will
be rectified in subsequent printings if notice is given to the
publisher.

All the Internet addresses (URLs) given in this book were valid
at the time of going to press. However, due to the dynamic
nature of the Internet, some addresses may have changed, or
sites may have changed or ceased to exist since publication.
While the author and Publishers regret any inconvenience this
may cause readers, no responsibility for any such changes can
be accepted by either the author or the Publishers.

Contents

Throughout this book, you will find green text boxes that contain facts and questions to help you interact with a primary source. Use these questions as a way to think more about where our historical information comes from.

Some words are shown in bold, **like this**. You can find out what they mean by looking in the glossary, on page 46.

Why Did We Fight the Revolutionary War?

Today, the United States of America is one of the strongest nations in the world. This makes it difficult to imagine how close the American **colonies** were to failing in their revolution. The supporters of the Declaration of Independence risked their lives in a **rebellion** against the most powerful nation in the world in 1776.

In 1760, George III became king of Great Britain. He signed the Treaty of Paris with France in 1763 to end the **French and Indian War**. The British gained control of Canada and the land east of the Mississippi River. However, Great Britain had a large debt from the war.

George III was 22 years old when he became king of Great Britain.

HIS MOST GRACIOUS MAJESTY KING GEORGE THE THIRD.

British Acts

King George III and the British **Parliament** believed that colonists in North America should help pay for the French and Indian War and the protection provided by British troops. They passed acts (laws) that required the colonists to pay taxes. The colonies responded by protesting and **boycotting** British goods. Colonists formed groups such as the **Sons of Liberty** to take action against the acts.

Events turned violent in Boston in 1770. British troops fired on a rowdy crowd that was protesting British taxes. Samuel Adams called it the "Boston Massacre." He used the event to gain support for American independence from Great Britain. King George III ordered General Thomas Gage to use military force to keep Britain's authority and control in Massachusetts. In 1775, months before the signing of the Declaration of Independence, the Revolutionary War began.

EARLY FIGHTING

Many military events took place before the colonies declared their independence in 1776:

Battles of Lexington and Concord (April 1775)

British surrender at Fort Ticonderoga (May 1775)

Battle of Bunker Hill (June 1775)

Battle of Quebec, Canada (December 1775)

Siege of Boston and British evacuation (March 1776)

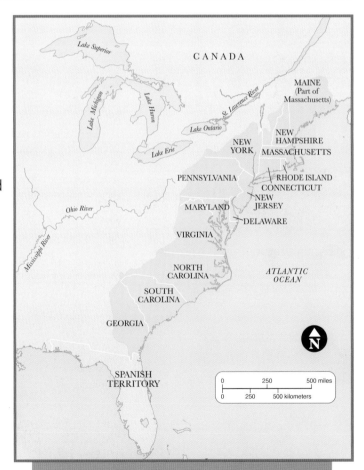

The boundaries of the original thirteen colonies were a bit different from how the states look today. Virginia was the first permanent European settlement in 1607, and Georgia was the last colony settled in 1733.

How Did the British Rule the Colonies?

The British king and **Parliament** ruled the **colonies** of North America from thousands of miles away. The king sent governors to the thirteen colonies. They made sure local communities obeyed the king's laws. Colonists participated in making some local laws. By the 1760s, the British government was more interested in the money it could make from the colonies to help pay its debt.

Taxes

In the past, the British did not directly tax the colonists. Some people felt it would be a violation of the colonists' rights, since they did not have representation, or a voice, in Parliament. However, the king and Parliament were determined to make the colonists help pay Britain's debt from the **French and Indian War**. Parliament ordered the colonies to pay several new taxes. In order for Britain's **merchants** and government to collect all profits, the British also continued to insist that colonial goods be shipped only to Great Britain and its **territories**.

> **RESTRICTING WESTWARD EXPANSION**
>
> King George III issued the Proclamation of 1763. It was meant to stop settlers from expanding west of the Appalachian Mountains. That land was reserved for Native Americans of the region. Colonists felt the king had no right to restrict them from moving. They ignored the proclamation. Settlers continued to expand west, threatening Native Americans as they moved into their territories.

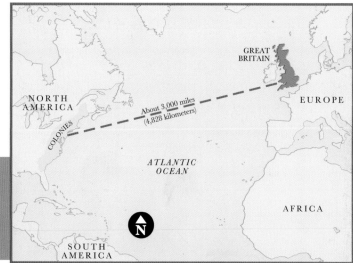

In the late 1700s, it could take two months to travel by sea between the colonies and Great Britain.

The Sugar Act

The Sugar Act of 1764 collected taxes on molasses. It also made it illegal for Americans to import molasses from other countries. The British went from controlling trade in the colonies, to raising money directly from them. Colonists such as Samuel Adams spoke out against the Sugar Act. The colonists said the act violated their rights because it was a tax without colonial agreement or representation in Parliament. Colonial business owners and merchants were concerned about the effect the tax would have on trade and the economy.

Primary Source:
Tax Stamp (1765–1766)

Tax stamps issued by the British government were used to stamp papers to prove the tax had been paid.

Thinking About the Source:

What do you notice first about this stamp?

What, if any, words can you read in this image?

The Stamp Act

In March 1765, **Parliament** approved the Stamp Act. This required colonists to purchase a stamped paper as a tax along with any printed materials. This included legal forms. But it also included newspapers, and even playing cards. Protestors from almost all parts of American society organized resistance to the Stamp Act. Some men formed secret organizations called the **Sons of Liberty** to oppose the act.

The Boston Massacre

The Townshend Acts of 1767 placed more taxes on goods coming into the **colonies**. Massachusetts resisted the taxes. The British sent troops to Boston to protect tax collectors and keep order. On March 5, 1770, violent protestors in Boston threw rocks and dared British troops to fire. One soldier fired, and the rest began to shoot. Five people were killed. The event became known as the "Boston Massacre."

British Parliament is made up of two groups. One is called the House of Lords, and the other the House of Commons (pictured here).

This is an American cartoon from 1774. It shows the effects of the Intolerable Acts — the acts are fanning the flames already burning in the Colonies. To the right, King George III watches.

ACTS AND TAXES ON THE COLONIES

Proclamation of 1763: Meant to prevent settlement west of Appalachian Mountains.

Currency Act (1764): Prevented use of colonial currency in place of British.

Sugar Act (1764): Taxed molasses shipped to colonies and prevented importing of molasses from other countries.

Stamp Act (1765): Required tax to be paid on paper documents made or sold.

Quartering Act (1765): Required colonists to house and feed British troops.

Declaratory Act (1766): Stated British Parliament was the only authority that could make laws affecting the colonies.

Townshend Acts (1767): Placed taxes on items brought into the colonies.

Tea Act (1773): Named East India Company as the only company allowed to sell tea in the colonies, with Parliament collecting a tax.

Intolerable Acts (1774): Closed Boston Harbor until the citizens of Boston paid for tea destroyed in the Boston Tea Party. Ended self-rule by colonists in Massachusetts. Made it illegal to put British officials on trial in colonial courts. Extended border of Canada into area claimed by colonists.

9

The Boston Tea Party

With the Tea Act of 1773, the British East India Company was given a **monopoly** on the tea trade. Three ships arrived in Boston Harbor full of tea, forcing the collection of tea taxes. Samuel Adams and the **Sons of Liberty** were determined not to pay. The night of December 16, 1773, colonists boarded the British ships and dumped their cargo of tea into Boston Harbor. This event became known as the Boston Tea Party.

Continental Congress

The British **Parliament** passed the Coercive Acts in 1774 in response to the Boston Tea Party. They closed Boston Harbor and were determined to make the colonists pay for the tea they destroyed. The first **Continental Congress** met in Philadelphia in response to these acts, which colonists called the "Intolerable Acts." Congress **asserted** the rights of the **colonies** and decided to discontinue all trade with Great Britain.

The second Continental Congress met in May 1775. It voted to start a Continental Army. George Washington was chosen as commander in chief. Congress created a post office to make communication among the colonies easier. It also created the Continental Navy. Congress appointed people to meet with Native Americans to ensure their peace with colonists.

Some colonists involved in the Boston Tea Party dressed as Mohawk American Indians.

Declaration of Independence

On June 11, 1776, the Continental Congress appointed a committee to write a declaration of independence from Great Britain. Thomas Jefferson wrote the declaration and revised it based on suggestions by John Adams and Benjamin Franklin. **Delegates** debated the wording for days. On July 4, the Continental Congress approved the Declaration of Independence. Washington's army now had a clear cause for which to fight.

THOMAS PAINE'S *COMMON SENSE*

Thomas Paine published a 50-page pamphlet called *Common Sense*. It outlined the reasons the colonies should separate from Great Britain and create their own government. *Common Sense* sold over 100,000 copies. It made the cause of independence popular. Paine's ideas influenced Thomas Jefferson, who later wrote the Declaration of Independence.

Primary Source:
The Declaration of Independence

This is an engraving of the signing of the Declaration of Independence.

Thinking About the Source:

What is the physical setting of this image?

Find something small, but interesting, in the image.

What Was Life Like on a New England Farm?

During the 1770s, most colonial farms were within 161 kilometers (100 miles) of the Atlantic Ocean. Settlers depended on fresh water and trees to grow or build what they needed. **Livestock** provided families with eggs, meat, milk, leather, and wool. Many farmers grew extra grains, vegetables, or fruits to sell in towns. Many colonial farmers joined state **militias**. If a farmer went to war, his wife and children took care of the farm.

Food for the Armies

During the Revolutionary War, farmers sold their crops to both armies. Sometimes they were promised payment that never came. Over time, British money was preferred over Continental dollars, which gradually became worthless by 1780. If a farmer got caught with a large amount of money from one side or the other, he could be tried for **treason** by the opposing side. The farmer could be put in jail, have his property taken away, or even be killed for supporting one of the armies.

Most farmers did not have slaves or indentured servants. Everyone, including children, pitched in with the farm work.

Outdoor Farm Duties

Men and boys did most of the outside work on the farm. Men cleared fields of stones and weeds, planted and harvested crops, cared for livestock, cut wood, and built fences and buildings. Plowing a new field often required moving heavy stones out of the way, chopping down trees, and pulling out stumps.

Women helped the men in the fields, especially during harvest time. They also tended, or took care of, vegetable gardens and milked cows. Children helped with the chores from a very young age. They chopped wood, gardened, gathered eggs, milked cows, and helped with other jobs around the farm.

Some small farmers could afford horses or oxen to help with work.

13

Indoor Farm Duties

Inside the home, women cleaned, cooked meals, spun thread and wove cloth, and raised the children. They also preserved fruits and vegetables for the winter, dried herbs for seasoning and medicine, and smoked meat so that it would keep longer. There was no refrigeration to keep food from spoiling, except for using large blocks of ice from frozen lakes and rivers.

Children helped keep the house clean. Boys chopped and brought in wood. A constant supply of wood was needed to keep the fire going. The fire was used for cooking, warmth, and cleaning clothes. Older children helped their mothers with cooking. Girls helped with sewing. All clothes and bedding were made by hand. All members of a farm family helped keep the farm running.

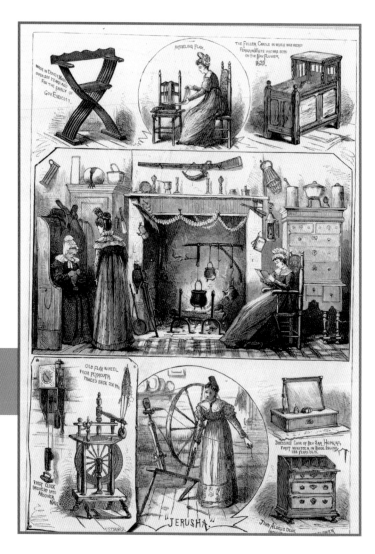

These illustrations show common items and scenes of a New England farmhouse in 1776.

CONSTANT WORK

Parson Smith of Connecticut served as a chaplain (religious leader) for the Continental force that seized Fort Ticonderoga in 1775. His wife, Mrs. Smith, spoke of life on the home front while her husband was away. Goods were in short supply. There was always work to be done:

"…all had to be raised and manufactured at home, from bread stuffs, sugar, and rum to the linen and woolen for our clothes and bedding… I rose with the sun and all through the long day I had no time for aught but my work… I was often wondering whether Polly had remembered to set the sponge [dough] for the bread, or to put water on the **leach tub**, or to turn the cloth in the **dying vat**, or whether wool had been carded [combed and prepared] for Betsy to start her spinning wheel in the morning, or Billy had chopped light wood enough for the kindling, or dry hard wood enough to heat the big oven, or whether some other thing had not been forgotten of the thousand that must be done without fail."

Women did most of the work in the home. There was rarely a moment to rest.

15

What Was Life Like on a Southern Plantation?

There were many small farms and businesses in the southern **colonies**, just like in the northern colonies. Large farms, called plantations, were common in the southern colonies. Plantations grew large amounts of crops to sell. Tobacco, rice, sugar, and **indigo** were popular **cash crops** grown on southern plantations. Northern colonies, Europe, and the West Indies (islands in the Caribbean Sea) purchased these crops.

Slave Labor

Many people were needed to work on the plantations. Plantation owners bought slaves to work in the fields. They hired white men to manage the slaves and carry out the planting of the crops. Most early battles of the Revolutionary War were fought in the North. As the war continued, fighting moved south. Plantations were damaged. Some **Patriots** abandoned their plantations when the British arrived. Sometimes they took their slaves. Other times slaves were left alone to try to survive.

The agricultural South depended on slave labor. Without modern equipment, harvesting cash crops required the hard work of many people.

Women in Charge

Wives of plantation owners managed the household. They planned meals, arranged social activities, supervised the children, and directed the slaves who worked inside the house. Men usually managed the money and other business matters. However, when the men were fighting in the Revolutionary War, women took over management of plantations.

Children

Children often helped with chores such as cooking or cleaning. They did little work overall, since plantations used slaves. Plantations were located in the countryside. Private tutors (teachers) were hired to teach the children of the plantation at home.

Plantations were small, self-contained cities. A plantation might have a stable for horses, school for the children, and mill for grinding grain.

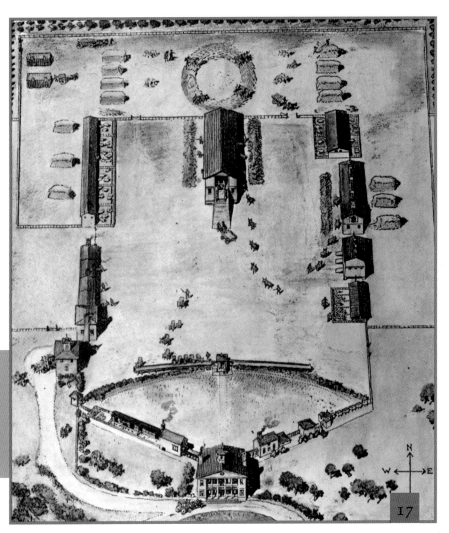

Nancy Hart took British soldiers by surprise and held them captive until help arrived.

PLUNDERING OF PLANTATIONS

Plundering, or stealing, by soldiers was common during the Revolutionary War. When men were away, southern plantations made rich targets. Women, children, and servants lived in fear of soldiers who might steal and destroy plantation property, or worse. Despite that fear, some women helped one side or the other when they could. Eliza Wilkinson was a **Patriot** left in charge of a plantation in South Carolina. She recalled a visit by plundering British troops during the war:

> "…I heard the horses of the inhuman Britons coming in such a furious manner that they seemed to tear up the earth… They were up to the house—entered with drawn swords and pistols in their hands…

> They then began to plunder the house of every thing they thought valuable or worth taking… I ventured to speak to the inhuman monster who had my clothes. I represented to him the times were such we could not replace what they'd taken from us, and begged him to spare me only a suit or two; but I got nothing but a hearty curse for my pains…

> The other wretches were employed in the same manner; they took my sister's earrings from her ears… They demanded her ring from her finger. She pleaded for it, told them it was her wedding ring, and begged they'd let her keep it. But they still demanded it, and, presenting a pistol at her, swore if she did not deliver it immediately, they'd fire."

Wealthy plantation owners could afford nice clothes. They also had time to enjoy music and other fun activities, since slaves did most of the hard work.

What Were Colonial Cities Like?

The most populated cities of North America were in the northeast. In 1760, about 23,000 people lived in Philadelphia, Pennsylvania. Other large cities included New York City and Boston, Massachusetts. Charleston, South Carolina, was the most populated city in the South. Valuable goods came and went from these busy seaports. During the Revolutionary War, the British fought the Americans for control of these cities.

The People

Many different classes of people lived in cities during the war. Wealthy citizens were often **merchants** who owned large businesses. These men were usually educated and often participated in **politics**. Middle-income citizens were usually craftsmen who owned small businesses or were laborers for larger businesses. Slaves or **indentured servants** worked for wealthier citizens.

Boston, Massachusetts, was one of the most populated cities in the northeast. A view of the old statehouse in Boston is pictured here.

Clothing

Style was important for the wealthy. Men wore breeches, or short pants, that buttoned below the knee. They tucked long, woolen stockings under the breeches. They wore long suit coats or waistcoats over loose-fitting shirts. Men grew their hair longer and wore it in a ponytail.

Women wore long dresses, often covering them with aprons to protect them. Dresses for special occasions were often made of silk and had layers of petticoats (thin skirts) underneath. Middle-income adults dressed similarly to the wealthy. However, the cloth they used was less expensive. Children's clothing looked like their parents' clothing. Slaves and servants dressed in poorer quality material that cost less money.

Education

Wealthy people often sent their sons to private schools or hired tutors. Some girls attended school, but most were taught at home. Girls usually learned only the skills needed to be good wives and mothers. In most middle-income families, mothers taught these skills to their daughters. Some less wealthy city children went to public schools. Slaves and indentured servants did not attend school.

**Primary Source:
Colonial Printing Press**

Printing presses were used to print newspapers. There were as many as 40 newspapers in the colonies at the time of the Revolutionary War.

Thinking About the Source:

What do you notice first about this object?

What can you learn from examining this object?

Philadelphia Grows and Develops

Philadelphia, Pennsylvania, was a typical large city of the late 1700s. It had **cobblestone** streets and brick sidewalks. Streetlamps brightened walkways at night. Homes were made of brick, stone, or wood. None had running water or indoor bathrooms. People kept **livestock** in their yards. There were public schools, a museum, a public library, and a medical school. People could attend the theater. A hospital was available for medical emergencies. A prison housed criminals.

By 1776, more than 30,000 people lived in Philadelphia. It was a busy port city. Farmers delivered their crops to **merchants**. The merchants shipped the crops to other **colonies**, Europe, or the Caribbean. As the city grew larger, workers were needed to construct buildings. Craftsmen were needed to make furniture and decorative items, especially for wealthier citizens. A variety of other businesses, such as fishing, shipbuilding, and whaling, also did well.

Philadelphia During the War

Philadelphia's large size and central location made it an important meeting place during the Revolutionary War. A state house, later named Independence Hall, was a center for government activity. The **Continental Congress** met there and approved the Declaration of Independence.

During the war, British naval **blockades** disrupted activities. Trade continued, but costs were much higher. Colonists fought hard to keep Philadelphia from British control at the Battles of Brandywine, Germantown, and Trenton. However, the British occupied the city from 1777 to 1778.

Some people in Philadelphia welcomed the arrival of the British. In June 1778, the British left the city, along with about 3,000 **Loyalists**.

Taverns and inns were also known as public houses. They offered food and a place to sleep for travelers. They also served as meeting places, where men discussed the issues of the day.

Did Everyone Support the War Against the British?

At the beginning of the Revolutionary War, there were three almost equally divided groups of people in the **colonies**: **Patriots**, **Loyalists**, and those who remained neutral (did not choose a side). Colonists who supported the British were called Loyalists. They did not want the government to change. Those who supported independence from Great Britain were called Patriots.

Who Were the Loyalists?

Loyalists came from all parts of colonial society. Wealthy **merchants** who did not want their businesses to change became Loyalists. Slaves who joined the British military to win their freedom were Loyalists. Some Loyalists acted as spies or served in the British military. Others lived quietly, not wanting to risk injury or death.

Loyalists were sometimes tarred and feathered and embarrassed by local Patriots. Where loyalists were greater in number, Patriots were often treated in a similar way.

LIBERTY TREE

Were Loyalists a Threat?

Patriots often mistreated Loyalists. Despite the fears Loyalists faced, many did help the British. Some spied for the British. Some fought for the British Army. Others sold food and supplies to the British. In a letter in 1777, Samuel Adams discussed the Loyalist threat:

"In my opinion, much more is to be apprehended [feared] from the secret machinations [plans] of these rascally people [the Loyalists] than from the open violence of British and Hessian soldiers, whose success has been in a great measure owing to the aid they have received from them [the Loyalists]."

STAYING NEUTRAL

Peter Van Schaack was a New Yorker who saw both sides of the argument. He felt British taxes had gone too far. However, he also felt independence was extreme:

"...I cannot see any principle of regard for my country which will authorize me in taking up arms, as absolute *dependence* and *independence* are two extremes which I would avoid; for, should we succeed in the latter, we shall still be in a sea of uncertainty and have to fight among ourselves for that constitution we aim at."

Many colonists protested British taxes and refused to buy British goods. The Stamp Act was especially unpopular, and colonists in Boston protested by burning Stamp Act papers.

Treatment of Loyalists

There were many **Loyalists** throughout the **colonies**. Some were rich and in positions of power. **Patriots** saw them as a threat to the cause of independence from Great Britain. Colonies passed laws requiring people to prove their devotion (dedication) to independence by taking an oath of loyalty. They also created penalties against being loyal to King George III. Colonies could impose heavy taxes on loyalists. A loyalist's property could be taken away, and the person could be **banished**.

Liberty organizations in cities and towns worked to scare Loyalists. Tarring and feathering was a popular way to do this. A person would be stripped, covered in tar, covered in feathers, and then carted around town for all to see. Usually the person was not seriously injured. However, some loyalists were put in prison, or rarely even put to death. After the war, up to 100,000 Loyalists left the colonies to live in Britain, Canada, or British **territories**.

TARRING AND FEATHERING

A man named Alexander Graydon recalled how a loyalist named Doctor Kearsley was tarred and feathered in Philadelphia in 1775:

"He was seized at his own door by a party of the **militia**, and, in the attempt to resist them, received a wound in his hand from a **bayonet**. Being overpowered, he was placed in a cart provided for the purpose, and amidst a multitude of boys and idlers, paraded through the streets to the tune of the rogue's march. I happened to be at the coffee-house when the concourse arrived there. They made a halt, while the Doctor, foaming with rage and indignation, without his hat, his wig dishevelled and bloody from his wounded hand, stood up in the cart…

What were the feelings of others on this lawless proceeding, I know not, but mine, I must confess, revolted at the spectacle. I was shocked at seeing a lately respected citizen so cruelly vilified…"

REPRESENTATION DU FEU TERRIBLE A NOUVELLE YORCK

Schröckenvolle Feuersbrunst welche zu Neu York von denen Americanern in der Nacht vom 19 Herbst Monath 1776 angeleget worden, wodurch alle Gebäude auf der West Seite der neuen Börse, längst der Broockstrent biß an das Königl Kollegii mehr als 1600 Häuser, die Dreyfaltigkeits Kirche, die Lutherische Kapelle u. die armen Schule in Asche verwandelt worden.

Representation du Feu terrible a Nouvelle Yorck que les Americains ont allumé, pendant la Nuit du 19 Septembre 1776 par le quel ont été brulés tous les Batiments du Coté de Ouest, à droite de Börse dans la Rue de Broock jusqu'au Collège du Roi et plus que 1600 Maisons avec l'Eglise de la St. Trinité la Chapelle Lutherienne et L'Ecole des pauvres

Primary Source:
New York City Fire, 1776

When the British moved in to occupy New York, the city was set on fire. It was never determined which side actually started the blaze.

This hand-colored etching shows buildings on fire and citizens being beaten by the British soldiers on September 19, 1776. It was created in 1778, two years after the events.

Thinking About the Source:

Describe what you see in this image.

Why do you think this image was made?

The text below the image is actually in German and French. It is a list of some of the institutions that were destroyed by the fire.

Does this change why you think the image was made?

What Role Did Blacks Play During the Revolution?

In the 1700s, slavery was legal in the **colonies**. **Merchants** made large profits from buying and selling slaves taken by force from Africa. During the Revolutionary War, there were over 400,000 slaves living within the colonies. Most of them worked the fields on southern plantations. Slaves also worked as servants in cities and towns.

Black families were often separated when sold at slave **auctions**. By law, anyone born to a slave automatically became a slave. Even though slaves were valuable, they were treated poorly. They did not have any legal rights. Sometimes their masters beat them, or worse. They received no formal education. Few had any hope of ever being anything but a slave.

Slaves Fight for the Colonies

At the beginning of the war, slaves freed by their owners could volunteer to fight. Southern representatives to the **Continental Congress** were against allowing slaves in the Continental Army. George Washington was ordered to stop **enlisting** slaves. As the war went on, the Continental Army was in great need of soldiers. Congress finally offered freedom to slaves if they served in the army.

More than 5,000 Africans, including slaves and free men, joined the Continental Army. Some slave owners who joined the army took their slaves with them. Others sent slaves in place of their sons. In the South, many owners did not want their slaves to go to war. They were too valuable to risk losing.

Privateers

Escaped slaves and former slaves often found work as sailors on the crews of fishing and whaling boats, as well as merchant ships. Many blacks became **privateers** during the Revolutionary War. Privateers were not part of the Continental Navy, but they worked to hurt British shipping and trade around the colonies.

The just man shall be in eternal remembrance

The brave Soldier of the Revolutionary War 1770.

Crispus Attucks

Crispus Attucks was a black sailor who worked on a whaling ship. Attucks was one of the people killed at the Boston Massacre in 1770.

Spies

Some blacks worked as spies. James Armistead was a slave. He got permission from his owner to join the Continental Army. In 1781, his commanding officer was the Marquis de Lafayette. Lafayette asked Armistead to go into a British Army camp and pretend he wanted to help the British. He sent information about British troops to the Continental Army.

After a time, British General Cornwallis asked Armistead to spy on Lafayette and the Continental Army. Armistead remained loyal to the **Patriots**. He gave false information to the British, while continuing to spy for Lafayette. After the Revolutionary War, in 1786, Armistead finally received his freedom.

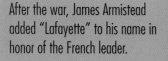
After the war, James Armistead added "Lafayette" to his name in honor of the French leader.

Slaves Fight for the British

More slaves fought for Great Britain than for the **colonies**. The British offered freedom to slaves who joined their army or navy. Many slaves escaped from plantations to gain freedom. Some slaves helped the British Army by serving as guides in unfamiliar countryside. Others served as cooks and took care of the horses.

After they won the war, colonists demanded that Great Britain return all American property. This included runaway slaves, whom they considered to be property. The acting commander of the British Army refused to do this. Many slaves who had fought for the British during the war boarded British ships and traveled to British **territories** to begin new lives.

Against Slavery

During the Revolutionary War, more colonists began to feel that slavery was morally wrong and should be abolished (done away with). As white colonists debated human rights and independence, more saw clearly how unfair it was that slaves had neither of these things.

THE BLACK REGIMENT OF RHODE ISLAND

With the need for more Continental troops, some colonies began recruiting black soldiers. In February 1778, Rhode Island decided to create a new 1st regiment. Free blacks and slaves were allowed to join, as well as Native Americans. Rhode Island paid owners for their slaves. The black volunteers received the same pay as white soldiers. More importantly, they were given their freedom.

The Black Regiment of Rhode Island became a trained fighting force. The black soldiers successfully fought against professional British and Hessian forces in the war.

What Role Did Native Americans Play During the Revolution?

As the **colonies** grew, Native Americans moved inland to less-settled land. This land was considered wilderness, even though it was barely 161 kilometers (100 miles) from the Atlantic Ocean. During the Revolutionary War, both the colonists and British wanted the support of Native Americans.

Fighting for the British

Most tribes did not choose a side in the Revolutionary War. The tribes that did choose usually fought for the British. About 13,000 Native Americans fought for the British. Many of them had fought for the British in the **French and Indian War**. Native Americans expected the British to win the Revolutionary War, because they had won the French and Indian War.

The British did not allow colonists to settle west of the Appalachian Mountains. The Native Americans were in favor of this because they did not want to lose any more of their land. A British victory in the revolution seemed like the best chance at preserving their traditional way of life.

British General John Burgoyne is pictured here speaking to Native Americans. Most Native Americans who fought in the Revolutionary War chose to fight for the British.

Fighting for the Colonies

Colonial leaders worked to establish peaceful relationships with the Native Americans. The colonies did not want to be fighting the Native Americans and British at the same time. Representatives from Congress convinced many Native Americans to remain neutral. A few hundred from the Oneida tribe joined the colonial side.

Some Tuscarora warriors also fought against the British. The Iroquois Confederacy, a group of six nations or tribes, was permanently divided because of the Revolutionary War.

TRIBAL LOYALTIES

Choctaw	British
Creek	British
Cherokee	British
Delaware	British
Shawnee	British

Iroquois Confederacy

Cayuga	British
Mohawk	British
Oneida	Colonial
Onondaga	British
Seneca	British
Tuscarora	Colonial

Joseph Brant was a Mohawk chief born in Ohio. His birth name was Thayendanegea. During the Revolutionary War, Brant convinced many Mohawks and other Iroquois tribes to support the British. He led raids (attacks) on **Patriot** settlers in an effort to keep them from taking more land.

33

Fighting on the Frontier

Fighting along the **frontier** was brutal. In the north, in Pennsylvania, New York, and Canada, some British encouraged Native Americans to spare no one in their fights against the colonists. There were Iroquois attacks against whole families of settlers. Colonial forces responded by burning entire tribal villages and fields of crops.

TECUMSEH.

Tecumseh was a teenager from the Shawnee nation during the Revolutionary War. He fought for the British against the colonists.

The Northwest frontier was part of the area now called the Midwest. During the Revolutionary War, Native-American warriors fighting for the British attacked frontier settlements and farms in the Northwest. In 1778, George Rogers Clark led 200 Long Knives into the wilderness of the Northwest. The Long Knives fought Native Americans who were British **allies**. They also captured British forts and trading posts.

Results of the War

At the end of the Revolutionary War, Native Americans faced a situation that was worse than ever. Most tribes had sided with the defeated British. They were treated as conquered people without rights by the new American government. Settlers continued to move farther west. Most Americans claimed the right to settle anywhere east of the Mississippi River. Native Americans continued to fight for their way of life.

BRUTALITY ON BOTH SIDES

Native-American allies of the British carried out vicious raids on frontier settlements. Colonial forces and **militia** responded with equal violence. British Colonel Henry Hamilton recorded what George Rogers Clark's men did to some Native Americans they captured:

> "The rest were surrounded and taken bound to the village where, being set in the street opposite the fort gate, they were put to death, notwithstanding a truce at that moment existed… One of them was **tomahawked** immediately… The rest underwent the same… One only was saved by the intercession of a rebel officer who pleaded for him, telling Colonel Clark that the savage's father had formerly saved his life."

In July 1778, British Colonel John Butler led a Native-American and **Loyalist** force in the Battle of Wyoming. The British won.

What Was Life Like for Women During the Revolution?

During the 1770s, colonial women were expected to care for their children and manage their households. This included the cooking, cleaning, and management of indoor servants or slaves. Most women did not receive much education, if any. Colonial laws were similar to British laws. Colonial women were not allowed to vote.

Some colonial women tried to continue with everyday life during the Revolutionary War. Many women took an active part in the war. Some women hoped the freedoms the **colonies** were fighting for would also apply to them. Abigail Adams was one such woman. Her husband, John Adams, served in the **Continental Congress**.

Abigail Adams believed women should not have to follow laws they played no part in making. After all, this idea contributed to the colonists' fight for independence.

Supporting the British Army

Some women helped the British Army during the Revolutionary War. Women called camp followers traveled with British troops doing laundry, mending clothes, cooking, and nursing the wounded. Some women acted as spies for the British. After the war, many of these women went to live in British **territories**.

Supporting the Colonial Army

Some women camp followers joined the colonial troops on the fighting fields to cook and do laundry for them, as well as act as nurses. Others, such as Deborah Sampson and Rachel and Grace Martin, disguised themselves as men and joined the army. Several women, such as Lydia Darragh, were spies.

When men were away fighting during the war, women took up doing a lot of the work on a farm.

Avoiding British Goods

At the time of the Revolutionary War, many goods were brought into the **colonies** from British territories. When the British began passing acts to tax colonists, **Patriots boycotted** British goods. Colonial women often purchased the goods for the household. Many did their part to protest British taxes and support independence by refusing to buy British goods, including tea. Patriotic women also gathered in groups called "spinning bees," to spin thread and weave cloth rather than purchase British fabric and clothing.

Spies and Messengers

Some women acted as spies during the Revolutionary War. Lydia Darragh and Sybil Ludington are two famous Patriot spies. In 1777, the British controlled the city of Philadelphia. On the night of December 2, 1777, Lydia Darragh overheard their plan to attack Washington's army, which was about 13 kilometers (8 miles) away. Darragh obtained a pass to visit a nearby mill to get flour. Once out of the city, she was able to pass a message to warn Washington about the attack.

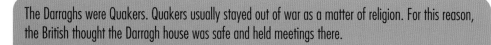

The Darraghs were Quakers. Quakers usually stayed out of war as a matter of religion. For this reason, the British thought the Darragh house was safe and held meetings there.

Colonel Henry Ludington commanded the local **militia** in his county. In April 1777, the British invaded Connecticut and were ordered to burn Danbury, where the Patriots had supplies stored. The colonel's daughter, Sybil, had just turned 16. She rode on horseback through the night to tell the militiamen to meet at their house by daybreak. By dawn, most of the militiamen were gathered and ready to march.

Ann Bates and her husband stayed loyal to the British. During the Revolutionary War, Bates pretended to be a traveling saleswoman. She sold items such as thread and cooking pots to camp followers of the Continental Army. As she sold items in the camps, Bates gathered information about Continental troops to give to the British.

Sybil Ludington road all night 64 kilometers (40 miles) across the countryside to alert the local militiamen.

Sybil Ludington

What Were Children Doing During the Revolution?

Boys under the age of 16 were technically not allowed to join the army. However, some Continental soldiers during the revolution were 15 years old, or even younger. A ten-year-old boy named Israel Trask volunteered for the army along with his father. He served as a messenger and cook's helper.

Joining the Army

Colonial boys heard stories about fighting and heard adults talk about the war. Many of them craved adventure, not understanding how horrible war is. Some joined the army because their friends did. Joseph Plumb Martin was 15 when he volunteered for the Continental Army in July 1776. He kept a diary of his experience as a soldier.

Sometimes women and children became involved in fighting by defending their homes.

In one entry, Martin recalled how much he wanted to join the army when he was only 14 years old:

"I was ploughing in the field about half a mile from home…when all of a sudden the bells fell to ringing and three guns were repeatedly fired…down in the village… I set off to see what the cause of the commotion was. I found most of the male kind of the people together; soldiers for Boston were in requisition [demand]. A dollar deposited upon the drumhead was taken up by someone as soon as placed there, and the holder's name taken, and he enrolled with orders to equip himself as quick as possible… O, thought I, if I were but old enough to put myself forward, I would be the possessor of one dollar, the dangers of war to the contrary notwithstanding; but I durst not put myself up for a soldier for fear of being refused."

Many of the youngest boys in the Continental Army played the drum. The drum set the beat for soldiers while marching. It was also used to sound out signals and commands to be heard across the battlefield.

At Home

Children of small farms and households were expected to do a lot of work at a very young age. With the oldest men of the household off fighting in the war, children had even more work to do. Boys chopped wood and did the hard work in the fields, as well as tending **livestock**. Girls helped their mothers cook and clean, and also helped with the livestock.

Education

Some girls learned to read and write at home, if their mothers taught them. Most did not go to school. Boys were usually needed on the farms, but they sometimes attended schools, if their communities had one. Most boys only went to school until the age of 13. After that, a boy became an **apprentice** to a craftsman in order to learn a trade, or skill.

Children of colonial households were put to work at a very young age.

Boys from the upper class were well-educated. They learned Latin, ancient Greek, history, philosophy, geometry, **surveying**, and other subjects. A few went on to study at a college in the **colonies** or in Europe.

Samplers

Young girls learned all the jobs and chores of their mothers and helped them around the house. They learned to sew like their mothers. Girls made samplers to practice sewing. Samplers are pieces of cloth decorated with needlework. Girls practiced stitching simple designs and sayings.

ANDREW JACKSON'S CHILDHOOD EXPERIENCE

Andrew Jackson became the seventh president of the United States in 1829. During the Revolutionary War, he was a teenager. Jackson participated in a small fight and was captured. A British lieutenant tried to make Jackson clean his boots. When he refused, the lieutenant cut Jackson's arm with his saber (sword). Jackson spent two months in a British jail. He caught smallpox while in jail, but survived.

Few children were able to attend school. Some were lucky enough to attend one-room schools. Sometimes they had to walk miles to get there and bring firewood to help heat the school.

Timeline

1754–1763	French and Indian War
1764	Sugar Act passed
1765	Stamp Act passed
1765	Quartering Act passed
	Sons of Liberty formed
1766	Stamp Act repealed
	Parliament passes Declaratory Acts
1767	Townshend Acts passed
1768	British troops in Boston
1770	Boston Massacre (March 5)
1772	Boston Committee of Correspondence formed
1773	Tea Act passed
	Boston Tea Party (December 16)
1774	Intolerable Acts passed
	First Continental Congress meets
1775	Paul Revere and William Dawes warn colonists that the British are coming
	Battles of Lexington and Concord (April 19)
	Second Continental Congress meets
	Battle of Bunker Hill (June 17)
	George Washington appointed commander of Continental Army
	Defeat at Quebec (December 30)
1776	Thomas Paine writes *Common Sense*
	Siege of Boston ends
	Declaration of Independence signed (July 4)
	New York falls to the British
	Battle of Trenton, New Jersey (December 26)
1777	Battle of Princeton, New Jersey (January 3)
	Fort Ticonderoga falls to the British (July 5)
	Battle of Bennington (August 16)
	Battle of Brandywine (September 11)

Philadelphia falls to the British (September 26)

Battle of Germantown (October 4)

Battle of Saratoga (October 7)

British General Burgoyne surrenders (October 17)

Congress passes Articles of Confederation (November 15)

Winter of Washington's army at Valley Forge

1778	France declares war and joins the Patriot cause
	Battle of Monmouth Courthouse (June 28)
	Savannah captured by the British (December 29)
1779	George Rogers Clark captures Vincennes (February 25) in the Western frontier
	Naval battle of John Paul Jones's *Bonhomme Richard* against the British warship *Serapis* (September 23)
1780	Charleston, South Carolina, falls to the British (May 12)
	Battle of Camden (August 16)
	Battle of Kings Mountain (October 7)
1781	Battle of Cowpens (January 17)
	Articles of Confederation adopted by the states (March 1)
	Battle of Guilford Courthouse (March 15)
	Battle of Eutaw Springs (September 8)
	Cornwallis and the British surrender at Yorktown, Virginia (October 19)
1783	Treaty of Paris signed, ending the war (September 3)
	Continental Army disbanded, and Washington retires from the military
1785	Congress establishes dollar as official currency
1786	Shay's Rebellion
1787	Northwest Ordinance
	Constitutional Convention meets and Constitution signed (September 17)
1788	Federalist Papers
	Constitution is ratified
1789	First meeting of Congress
	George Washington sworn in as first president
1791	Congress adopts the Bill of Rights as the first ten amendments to the Constitution

Glossary

apprentice someone who works for a person for a period of time in order to learn a certain skill or job

assert stand up for the rights of a person or place

auction public meeting where property is sold to the person who offers the most money

banish not allow to live or stay in a particular place

bayonet long knife that is attached to the end of a rifle

blockade surrounding an area to stop people or supplies from coming or going

boycott refuse to buy something or do something as a way of protesting

cash crop crop such as tobacco, rice, or cotton that is grown in large amounts to be sold for cash

cobblestone small round stone set in the ground for a road surface

colony area that is under the political control of a more powerful country that is usually far away

Continental Congress group of men who represented the thirteen colonies during the time of the Revolutionary War

delegate someone elected or chosen to represent a group of people

dying vat very large container used to store liquid dye to color cloth

enlist time in the military; to enlist is to join the military

French and Indian War name for fighting that took place from 1754–1763 in North America between the French and the British

frontier area where not many people have lived before and not much is known about; the borderlands of a country

indentured servant person who came to America under contract to work for another person for several years

indigo plant from which blue dye is made

leach tub tub used to leach ashes and bark, which meant soaking chemicals from them using water

livestock animals such as cows, chickens, or sheep that are usually kept on a farm

Loyalist person who remained loyal to Great Britain during the Revolutionary War

merchant someone who buys and sells goods in large amounts

militia group of people who act as soldiers but are not part of the professional army

monopoly having complete control of something so that others cannot compete

Parliament main lawmaking group in Great Britain; made up of the House of Lords and the House of Commons

Patriot person who supported independence during the Revolutionary War

plunder steal money or property from somewhere while fighting in a war

privateer armed ship that attacks and robs enemy ships carrying goods; person serving on a privateer ship

rebellion organized attempt to change the government or leadership of a country by using violence

siege situation in which an army surrounds a place to try to gain control of it or force someone out of it

smallpox serious disease that causes spots, which leave marks on the skin

Sons of Liberty secret groups formed in the colonies before the Revolutionary War that included people who supported independence from Great Britain

survey examine and measure an area of land and record the information on a map

territory land that is controlled by a particular country or ruler

tomahawk light axe used by Native Americans

treason crime of being disloyal to a person's country or government

Find Out More

Books

Anderson, Laurie Halse. *Independent Dames: What You Never Knew About the Women and Girls of the American Revolution*. New York: Simon & Schuster Children's, 2008.

Murray, Stuart. *American Revolution*. New York: DK Children, 2005.

Schanzer, Rosalyn. *George vs. George: The American Revolution as Seen from Both Sides*. Des Moines, Iowa: National Geographic Children's Books, 2007.

Websites

http://www.historyforkids.org/learn/northamerica/after1500/history/revolution.htm
This site, run by Kidipede, provides all kinds of links discussing different ideas and events of the Revolutionary War.

http://www.pbs.org/ktca/liberty/
This PBS site discusses the American Revolution and matches a TV series aired by PBS called "Liberty! The American Revolution," which is also available on DVD.

http://kids.yahoo.com/directory/Around-the-World/Countries/United-States/History/Colonial-Life-(1585-1783)/American-Revolutionary-War
This Yahoo! Kids site has useful links to other sites that discuss the Revolutionary War.

DVDs

Liberty! The American Revolution (DVD). Hosted by news anchor Forrest Sawyer and narrated by Edward Herrmann. PBS DVD Video, 1997.

The Revolution (DVD). History Channel DVDs, 2006.

Index